T0063014

The
Enlightened
RELATIONSHIP

STEVE SMITH, LMFT

BALBOA.
PRESS
A DIVISION OF HAY HOUSE

Balboa Press books may be ordered through booksellers or by contacting:

Balboa Press
A Division of Hay House
1663 Liberty Drive
Bloomington, IN 47403
www.balboapress.com
1 (877) 407-4847

Cartoon illustrations created by Alif Firdaus Azis

Printed in the United States of America.

ISBN: 978-1-4525-1765-0 (sc)
ISBN: 978-1-4525-1766-7 (e)

Balboa Press rev. date: 07/16/2014

Contents

Dedication

To my wife Lisa and daughter Jordyn. I
love you with all of my heart and soul.

To all the authors and spiritual teachers who
had the courage to express their truth.

And to all of my clients who have allowed me to
participate in their journey of growth and becoming.

Preface

In the winter of 1982, a plane carrying 74 passengers crashed into the icy waters of the Potomac River in Washington, DC. Several of the passengers survived the crash but were stranded on wreckage and blocks of ice floating in the middle of the river. After nearly 20 minutes, rescue workers finally arrived by helicopter and began to airlift the survivors out. A lifeline was lowered to one of the survivors, Arland Williams, Jr., but instead of holding on and saving himself, he passed the rope to one of his fellow passengers. He did this several times, allowing for the others to be pulled to safety while he clung to the ice in freezing waters. By the time the helicopter returned for the final rescue, Arland was gone. He couldn't hold on any longer and slipped away into the frigid water. I will never forget the profound impact this event had on my twelve-year-old mind. The idea that a man (or woman) could give up their life for the sake of another filled me with awe. For most people, this was a demonstration of courage and bravery to the highest degree. And it certainly was that, but it was also an act of pure love that touched something deep within my heart. It was the same way I felt when I thought about other heroic figures who personified love, such as Jesus or Mother Theresa. What could possess someone to make a decision to do such a thing?

I understand now that Arland was able to transcend the grip of his ego, which is based on fear and survival, and listen to the call of the heart. I don't know exactly what transpired in his mind, but my guess is that he surrendered to his Spirit, and let love lead the way. He was likely "possessed" by the Spirit of Love, which is indestructible, limitless, fearless, and knows we are all connected. And today, while his body may no longer contain life, that Spirit lives on and continues to inspire others, including me.

Most of us are not called to give up our life for the sake of another, but if we listen carefully, we are called to set aside our ego for the sake of love every single day. The ego, in the way I am defining it, is the personality construct comprised of belief systems that keep us separate and ward off any threats to the individual personality. It cannot see beyond the physical body or the connections that exist at the level of Spirit. The idea of genuine love threatens the ego because love recognizes oneness, togetherness, and connectedness. The paradox is that individuality still exists in genuine love, but the ego cannot comprehend that. It is only interested in survival, protection, and maintaining separateness, none of which are characteristics of love. The heroes who can overcome and transcend this limitation, such as Arland, Jesus, and others like them, symbolize the willingness to give up the self (ego) for the love of another. And it is in this transcendence where we can all truly find our Selves.

This does not require some fantastic or life-threatening event, and we don't have to go far to search it out. We can do this every day and with the people that are right next to us. Our partners or spouses offer wonderful opportunities that challenge our ego on a daily basis. We tend to complain about these challenges, not realizing these are the very gifts that can lead us to our freedom.

Chapter 1

Struck by a Bolt of Love

Have you ever felt **It**? What is **It**? **It** is the unconditional love pulsating at the very core of your being. For many years I never even knew it existed. While in my mid-20s, I was contemplating some of the mysteries of life, and a bolt of love suddenly struck me. It felt as though my heart split open and pure love was being poured into it. At the same time something merged into my mind and I could "see" more clearly. However, it wasn't my physical eyesight that improved; it was more like an increased clarity of perception. It was as though I had woken up, even though I was already awake, or as if someone just removed the blurry glasses through which I perceived the world. In an instant I knew that deep within me was a pure loving Being, shining its light, and that it had been there all along, although I was unaware of it. I also knew that this loving Being was unlimited and eternal, and it was the source of my life! All I could do was sit there and shed tears of joy for hours because I had come "home."

Four years before this experience I was at the lowest point of my life, living in complete despair. I had graduated from college and had no clue what I was going to do or what I was even passionate about. I played football in college and like most players I had dreams of playing in the NFL. I made it to the NFL combine testing but was not drafted by any teams--and that was it. *Finito*! My football career was over after playing for 15 years, and it caused quite an identity crisis within me. I completely identified with being an athlete and now that it was gone a deep emptiness overtook me. Every day was a struggle just to get by.

I somehow managed to survive this period and slowly began working my way out of the depression. After a few years, I started taking better care of myself, exercising again and reading self-help books such as *The Road Less Traveled* by M. Scott Peck. I began contemplating some of the most profound questions in life. Who is God? Why are we here? Where are we going? What is love and what does it really mean to love someone? I was also questioning whether I should continue dating the woman I was seeing at the time because I wasn't sure about it. During this searching and questioning, I began feeling a presence inside of me offering guidance. This presence felt like very strong intuition, but more powerful and with more clarity than I had ever experienced. At one point it urged me to "put your ego aside and just love her unconditionally." To my logical mind this didn't make any sense. If I love unconditionally, which means without any conditions, without any expectations, won't I get hurt? This is asking me to take a huge leap of faith and step into unknown territory. My ego was screaming, "Are you crazy? That's a big risk!" I had never done or even considered something like that before.

Now you must understand what I was being asked to do. Yes, I did feel a fondness and a strong attraction toward her, but I wasn't being guided to love her in a romantic or attached kind of way. It wasn't a "falling in love" type of experience. The guiding presence wasn't saying love her so that I could get something from it. It didn't tell me to get out my checklist and make sure she had all the qualities I was looking for in a woman. No! *It was saying to love her for the sake of love itself.* Love her because she is a fellow soul on a journey through life who is worthy of love, and it is through love that we are all healed and uplifted. See the beauty and goodness in her no matter what she displays on the outside. Be willing to nurture her entire being: body, mind and spirit. Despite not really knowing how to do this and having initial reservations, I somehow said YES to this invitation to love unconditionally. Shortly after making this decision, maybe a week or two, I had the experience of being struck by the bolt of love. Yes, I fell completely in love, but not with the woman I was with at the time. I had fallen in love with God, Spirit, the Divine, the Self, the Universe, Creation, All-That-Is, whatever you wish to call it—the Source of all life. For a few months I had similar experiences, each one a further confirmation of the Divine source within me and within all of creation. I came to realize that one of our reasons for living is to remember how to love as it does --UNCONDITIONALLY. I decided then that I wanted to help others connect to their own divinity and express it in their lives, so I committed myself to doing just that.

During those months I felt virtually no fear. I had no reason to fear anything because I knew there was no real death, no real risk, and that I (the real me) could never really be hurt. This knowing allowed me to fearlessly love without conditions. I could see the divinity in others regardless of what they were showing on the outside. It was as though I could see right through the façade of issues, fears, and "faults" to the perfection within. The way I have come to understand this experience is that when I had the willingness and courage to love another unconditionally, it gave my heart "permission" to experience the unconditional love of Creation itself. I had been given a key that unlocked a treasure chest full of the greatest heirloom in the Universe—divine Love. My eyes were opened to a new way of being and a new way of relating that I so much want to share with you.

The realizations that I experienced can be summarized in the following way:

1. We are loved and supported unconditionally by Creation, God, Spirit, Source Energy, All-That-Is (or whichever name you prefer).
2. We are not separate from that which loves and supports us. We are a part of this Energy and a unique expression of it.
3. One path to realizing our connection to Spirit is through our relationships with others. Learning (or remembering) how to love as it does allows us to experience our connection to Spirit more fully.

The New Frontier for Love

The old model of relating is not working anymore—have you noticed? Yes, the divorce rates are high, but the more important issue is the level of dissatisfaction and lack of fulfillment in our relationships with significant others. Much of our dissatisfaction arises from limiting beliefs about our relationships and ourselves. Many of us are operating, consciously or unconsciously, from an outdated model that has many distorted premises at its core. We must discard this old way of being and embrace the emerging paradigm if we want our relationships to thrive in the way they were intended.

You can, and are meant to have, an extraordinary relationship. This may be hard to believe, particularly if you are experiencing difficulty in your relationship right now. But the truth is that we should not settle for anything less. Why should we spend another day of unhappiness in our relationship? Isn't our wellbeing too important and our life too short for that? Now, before you run off and try to find another partner, let me be clear that I'm speaking about your current relationship. Yes, it is possible to eventually decide that your current partner may not be a good match for what you desire in a relationship, but no matter how problematic your relationship seems right now, it can improve with your conscious effort.

The great news is that you have the power to change your current situation. Let me repeat, **YOU** have the power to change your situation. This is especially true if both you and your partner are making the effort to improve it. However, even if your partner does nothing, your relationship experience can improve. This is because we as individuals are much more empowered than we commonly believe.

The new frontier for love is The Enlightened Relationship. With it, we will understand that relationships with significant others serve as a wonderful opportunity for us to awaken and discover ourselves as well as our inherent divine love. We will know that we are much more than a physical body and that we have divine reSources within us.

We will understand that we are all connected by an unseen energy and that we are more powerful than we have been taught. We will inspire the best in each other as partners. The ideas presented in the Enlightened Relationship are nothing new; they have existed for ages. But the majority of our world has yet to fully apply and live these principles in our relationships. A paradigm shift is no easy undertaking because our assumptions and beliefs are rooted so deeply, but the joy and love we have the potential to experience will make this journey so worthwhile. Trust me!

Let me offer a word of caution before we take the plunge into the depths of love and metaphysics. You must be willing to explore the inevitable paradoxes along the way. We will encounter many principles that are true and yet seem to be contradictory on the surface. Can two statements that are apparently contradictory both be true? Yes and no. It depends on the level of consciousness, or awareness, in which the statements are perceived. When looking at a situation from one perspective in may appear that both statements cannot be true. But if a shift in consciousness occurs and greater awareness is gained, it can become clear that both are true.

Imagine you and I start from the same location and one of us walks East and the other walks West. At one level of awareness, which we will call "two dimensional," it appears that we are walking in opposite directions and getting further apart. If we shift to a "three dimensional" awareness and look at the situation from above, we could see that the Earth is round and that we are walking both away from each other and toward each other at the same time. The fact that we are moving further apart and closer together at the same time can only be perceived at the higher level of awareness. If we keep walking around the Earth, we will pass each other on the opposite side and eventually meet in the same location in which we began. This would not seem possible at the two dimensional level.

In the same way, spiritual truth often contains interesting paradoxes at its core. If we are contemplating these ideas and we don't quite grasp its truth, it usually means we haven't experienced the level of awareness required. We may have heard a particular spiritual truth repeated many times, but it won't have significant meaning until we have an experience that allows us to see it. Our consciousness is enhanced through our experience and we become able to perceive from this expanded view. So open your mind and be willing to play in the fields of paradox, and just remember--the more you know, the more you realize you don't know!

I Think, Therefore I Vibrate?

Have you ever heard a young child ask "why?" over and over again? "Daddy, why are there stars in the sky?" a child may ask. We explain it to the best of our ability and the child says again, "Why?" We then try to explain why, but the child wants to go deeper and asks again, "But why?" And the deeper we go into the 'why,' the more we realize we really don't know. I must confess that I am actually the child in this scenario, particularly when it comes to the human psyche and spiritual matters. I want to know why! So when I began to study psychology and found that conventional psychology could only take me so far, I took the next step into transpersonal psychology, and finally I had to delve into the study of metaphysics.

Some people associate the term 'metaphysics' with the paranormal, psychic phenomena, spirituality, and many other areas. For me, metaphysics is a philosophy that explains the nature, structure, and process of existence itself. Before embarking on the journey to The Enlightened Relationship, let's lay some groundwork so that we understand some fundamental metaphysical principles.

Years ago I was introduced to the theory that everything originates from nonphysical energy that is "vibrating" at a certain frequency. This energy is the precursor, or source, of everything in the physical world. We are formed by this energy. Our thoughts and emotions are also made of this energy. We are focusing, transmitting, and receiving the energy in every moment. While this was interesting to consider and maybe even true at the level of quantum physics, I didn't see how it was relevant in our relationships. It took me many years to understand why this concept was important in the way we related with each other. In fact, it wasn't until I experienced a true dark night of the soul and significant problems in my own relationship that I began to discover its importance. I was in a state of great confusion and despair, but this experience sparked a deep desire within me to truly understand what was really happening at a fundamental level. So I kept digging for answers and they slowly (oh so agonizingly slow!) began to emerge.

The metaphysical theory is that we are a unique expression of Universal Consciousness, which is the original energy. We have two selves as expressions of this energy, a Spirit Self (with nonphysical awareness) and a personal self. The Spirit Self represents our true, natural selves, and its energy vibrates at a high frequency. The energy of our true selves is being projected into and through the physical body and brain. Our personal self receives this energy and in every moment is either allowing it or resisting it in varying degrees. Our general frequency rises the more our personal self allows this energy. Conversely, our general frequency lowers the more our personal self resists the energy of our Spirit Self. Our frequency fluctuates constantly based on the degree to which we are allowing or resisting our natural energy to flow into and through us.

Thoughts also have energetic frequencies. Thoughts that are loving, joy-based, peaceful, etc., have higher frequencies. The degree of allowing our natural energy to flow and the quality of our thoughts are directly related. When we are allowing and vibrating at a high frequency, we then have access to those loving, peaceful, joy-based thoughts because we are in their range. Much like a light bulb on a dimmer switch, when the energy is allowed, it fully lights up; just like we do when we allow our natural energy to flow. It is no accident that expressions such as "letting your light shine" are indications that we are being our best, most loving selves. In those moments we are allowing the truth of who we are to be expressed. And in contrast, when the dimmer switch is turned down (more resistance), the light bulb reflects it by emitting less light--just as we do when we resist our natural selves. Any thought that limits or restricts us is resistance, and will cause our light to dim.

Imagine that we have a field of potential thoughts around us at all times. The type of thoughts that are "near" to us and that we can choose depends upon our frequency in the moment. We can only choose thoughts, and therefore experiences, that are resonating near our current frequency. This is similar to a television set where we can only watch the channel we are tuned into. If we want to watch a different show, we must tune to a different channel. As we allow or resist by thinking new thoughts, the field of potential thoughts changes based on our new frequency. If we resist and move down in frequency, the field of potential thought changes slightly to reflect it. If we continue resisting, we will move further down and only have access to more 'negative' thoughts. Please note that I am using the word *negative* not as a value judgment, but to represent a direction toward lower frequency thoughts. Thoughts and emotions that are of a lower frequency are quite valuable in that they indicate our degree of alignment.

Our thought habits play a crucial role in our vibration and the type of thoughts we can choose. The more we think a certain way the more likely we will continue to do so. We develop patterns in the brain that we habitually follow. Some of these patterns serve us while others don't, but we are not destined to stay stuck in the same pattern unless we choose that path. If we consistently work to change our thought habits and rewire our brains, we can create new patterns that are more aligned with our true selves.

In addition to vibrating at certain frequencies, beliefs and thoughts are also creative. More and more people are coming to realize that consciousness creates form, not the other way around. Another way to look at this is to say that beliefs are the building blocks of our experiences. Even though many of us are beginning to understand this idea in principle, applying it to our benefit can still be challenging. This is because it is a complete about-face to our old way of thinking. In the old paradigm, we thought that our beliefs originated *from* our experiences. In other words, the idea was that we have an experience and create beliefs based on our emotions and observations of that experience. This is similar to the scientific method, where we construct beliefs based on what we observe in an experiment. Now we must do an about-face and come to understand that the way we experience events and circumstances will reveal to us what we actually believe. Notice it is *the way we experience* the events and circumstances, such as our emotional reactions and judgments, which provides the most valuable information.

The stronger the belief, the more likely it will become a physical manifestation and an experience. The Universe is designed in such a way that our internal dialog (a blend of beliefs, expectations, perceptions, and thoughts) becomes our experiences. Every experience we have is a creation of ours based on how we have been thinking and the frequencies at which we have been vibrating. We transmit these signals to the Universe and the Universe responds by giving us experiences that match.

We have thousands of thoughts each day and all of our thoughts are not fully conscious, so we are not always aware of everything we are thinking. Some of our beliefs are so ingrained and assumed that they operate behind the scenes. We often have subconscious programs that operate much like malware on a computer. When we think about a certain subject, such as relationships, money, or health, the malware gets activated and begins running in our subconscious. This malware is why we sometimes create experiences we do not want. What we want to believe is not always what we actually believe. However, we can always look to our experiences to tell us exactly how we have been thinking and what we believe about our lives, because these experiences are a reflection of our internal dialogue.

Wouldn't it be great if everyone had frequency meters that were visible to the world at large? The meter would measure and display the degree to which we were allowing our natural energy to flow as a percentage. A reading of 100% would be the highest frequency and 0% the lowest. That way we would know the frequency of everyone around us. If we came across someone with a reading of 100% we would know in that moment they were aligned with their true Self. Of course, we can sometimes determine it by reading body language, actions, and facial cues, but having a number would be marvelous! I think we would notice that many of the people we interact with would have a similar meter reading.

Mirror, Mirror on the Wall

And how does this apply to our relationships? Am I making the unpopular proclamation that we, as individuals, create every experience in our relationships? Yes, I am. You may ask, '*How can I be creating these experiences when there is another person involved? I don't control their behavior.*' Nowhere is this concept more difficult to grasp than in our relationships. It seems to be much easier for us to understand how we create our experiences with money, for example, based on our beliefs and thoughts about prosperity, abundance, etc. If we have limiting beliefs about prosperity or habitual thoughts of lack, then we will struggle with feeling prosperous. And when we are single many of us can even understand the concept of "attracting" a partner based on the beliefs we hold about being in a relationship, being loveable, deserving to be in a relationship, etc. But when we are already in a relationship, it is often extremely difficult to recognize that we are creating our experiences with our partner based on our own internal beliefs and dialog.

What do you see when you look closely into the pupil of your partner's eyes? If you have never tried this exercise, please do so. When you look closely into the pupil of another's eyes you see a reflection of yourself. I do not believe that our eyes are designed as mirrors by accident. This represents a core truth about our relationships—that they are reflections of us. And I mean this in a very literal sense. The way we experience our partners is a direct reflection of our own internal experience. Many of us fall into a pattern of blaming our partners for our experiences. A pattern of blame is not only disempowering to us, but it is the equivalent of blaming a mirror for showing us our own reflection. We can scream and blame the mirror all we want, but if we don't change, the reflection cannot change. This is Universal Law. Once we truly understand and integrate this principle, we can transform our own consciousness and begin to see the reflection in our relationships.

Chapter 2

The Jerry McGuire Syndrome
to
Cultivating the Love Within

In the movie *Jerry McGuire,* there is a fantastic scene that epitomizes one of the central problems in our understanding of relationships. After being separated from his beloved, Jerry returns to her and in true romantic form proclaims, "You complete me." The women in the scene who are witnessing this romantic proclamation virtually melt in their seats. OK, I admit it. I love this scene too! We melt when we see it because it evokes such strong emotion. Those of us who have ever felt enthralled by our beloved can truly relate. However, we are in big trouble if we believe that someone completes us. What happens when they are not around? Are we not complete? What happens if they change? Do they still complete us? You can see the inherent problem of dependency in this misconception.

Then what about the feeling that Jerry and so many of us have experienced? Is it real? And most importantly, the million dollar question is, why doesn't it last? Well, the feeling is real and that is undeniable. Whatever words we want to use, love, bliss, ecstasy, etc., it is an incredible feeling to be in love. The problem arises from two assumptions we make. The first is that the feeling of being in love is somehow coming from the other person. The second assumption is that we need the other person in order to feel this way.

The truth is that the feeling is coming from within us, and our attention on the other person has caused us to allow these feelings to flow through our being. While we may want to attribute our good feeling to our partner, it is really something we are doing (unconsciously perhaps) that is allowing it within us. Very often we experience "falling" in love because the other person has characteristics, traits, and strengths that are underdeveloped in us, and we really do feel complete with them. They represent what we do not yet embody and we assign majestic status to them. When I first met my wife I was enthralled by her openness and gregarious personality, which were some of the qualities that were underdeveloped in me. I was then attracted to her for this reason, and she was attracted to my quietness and stability. So it is understandable that we would feel complete when we are with someone who embodies what we do not. The problem is that we deny or inhibit these qualities within ourselves and think we need the other to represent them.

There may be many other reasons we experience "falling" in love or feeling complete with another, such as having a past life connection or agreement that is being fulfilled. Another possibility is that this person may represent exactly what we have desired in a mate and the manifestation has now arrived. Whatever the reason, we are best served to see the experience as a gift that has ***awakened love within us***. Now that it is awake we can cultivate and allow that love to flow outward, not just to our beloved, but to all beings.

Let me be clear. I am not trying to kill romance. I think romance is wonderful and should be enjoyed to the fullest. Savor those feelings of being in love or even being complete, but recognize that the feeling is not originating from your partner and you do not need them to activate it—despite what every romantic comedy film has portrayed. It is astonishing that almost all films and television shows about love continue to propagate the idea that we need a certain person in order to be in a state of love. They imply that if we can just find the right person, we will then be able to love. The film industry is in large part just reflecting the beliefs we continue to hold in our mass consciousness. When we begin to shift our consciousness and definitions about loving relationships with significant others, we will see those changes in movies and television.

Cultivating the Love Within

Where is the feeling of being in love coming from if not from the other person? It comes from our own inner, true Self. This is because we are, at our core essence, pure loving energy. When we align with our true Self, we experience the feeling of love. Our minds and bodies translate this alignment with our true Self as the emotion of love. In terms of vibration, our true Self is pure-pristine-loving energy and is vibrating at the highest frequency. Our emotions are indicators of how closely our thoughts and frequency are in alignment with the true Self. For example, our true Self believes in us fully, knows we have unlimited potential and can achieve anything we truly desire. When we doubt ourselves or worry about our abilities, these thoughts are not aligned with our true Self and we experience uncomfortable feelings. Our true Self sees only the best in our partners and believes in them fully as well, because that is its nature. When we see only the best in our partners and believe in them, it feels so good because we are aligned with who we truly are. Our frequency then matches our higher Self's frequency and we are in a state of love. So the love we seek in our relationships is already within us. The first component to The Enlightened Relationship is to *cultivate the love that is within.*

As most of us have found through experience, it is much easier to do this at the beginning of a relationship. Without a long history with someone, we can see the best in him or her and judge them less. Over time it can become more challenging to focus in this way and we often experience being in love less and less. We begin resisting our true Self more and more.

In the case of the Jerry McGuire Syndrome, it's true that we are seeing the best in our partners, which is exactly what our true Self sees in them. In all of their imperfections they are perfect just as they are. We are aligning with the view of our true Self. What is missing in the Jerry McGuire Syndrome is the realization that the love is coming from within us and that we are also perfectly imperfect, even without them. We are projecting divinity onto our beloved without recognizing that *we are also divine.*

Love for Another is Self-Love

Have you ever tried to withhold love from your partner? Maybe you were angry about something they did or said and you made a deliberate effort not to show love. Did you notice how terrible this felt? The reason it feels terrible is that when we withhold love from our partners we are withholding it from ourselves. When we try to withhold love we are moving away from our true nature. I still find myself falling into this trap occasionally with my wife. I will be stewing over something she has done and have spiteful thoughts such as, 'Don't be nice to her,' or 'Don't show her any affection.' This is going against my very nature. If I want happiness, I have no choice but to move toward love. Sometimes it takes longer than others, but I must move in that direction if I want genuine happiness.

Consciously choosing to return to love is an act of self-love, even if the love is directed toward another. It is proclaiming that we care about ourselves so much that we will do everything we can to return to a loving state. The opposite is true as well. If we are resenting another person we are the ones experiencing resentment, so it is really self-resentment.

Take Your Emotional Vitamins

If we were to look at all of the emotional states in a range, we would have those that feel the best at the higher end. This would include emotions such as love, joy, appreciation, and passion. Moving downward, the range would progress toward emotions that feel less and less pleasurable. We would reach contentment and then eventually frustration, anger, and so on. At the bottom end we might have emotions such as terror, fear and despair. At any given point and time we are somewhere on this range, and as we move through life we go up and down in varying degrees. For the sake of simplicity, I have only chosen to place a few emotions in the range. There are, of course, many other emotions we could insert as well. The words I am using to describe the emotions are less important and the exact placement of a particular emotion is also not critical to this conversation. We may not even be able to identify the exact emotion we are experiencing, but we are always somewhere in the range. What is most important is to understand that we are either moving toward love or away from it at any given moment (i.e., toward alignment with our true Self or not).

Emotional State of Being

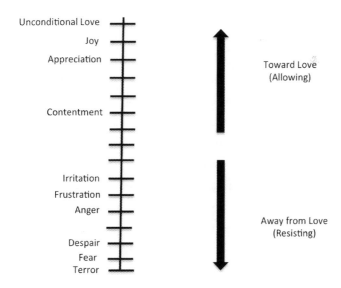

Where would we prefer to be on the scale? On the high end, of course, feeling love, joy, etc. because we are aligned with our true Self and it feels so good to be there. But that is not the only reason to be there. We are at our best when we are feeling good. We are a better partner, parent, worker, and creator. We are better at almost everything we do when we are feeling good. In addition, the human body functions more optimally the better we feel. Our bodies are designed to function better and more efficiently at all levels when we activate positive emotions. Spending time each day consciously feeling emotions such as appreciation, love, and peace is like taking emotional vitamins.

Let's consider this with respect to the brain and decision-making. If the brain is working more optimally and thinking more clearly when experiencing positive emotion, what should we do if we are trying to solve a problem or have an important decision to make? We should do our best to experience positive emotion so that the brain, and therefore our minds, can function optimally. If we were discussing an important issue, problem solving, or making a decision with our partners, it would be to our advantage to apply this concept. Many of us mistakenly believe that we should be "serious" when discussing important matters. Getting serious, in the sense that there is a kind of stress involved, actually constricts us and limits our ability to think freely and creatively. We can deem an issue very important and still feel relaxed and at ease in the conversation, which more closely aligns us with our true Self.

I'm Not in Love with My Partner

The reason many people decide to end relationships is because they are "not in love" with their partner anymore. Let's examine this with the ideas we have already discussed. We have stated that love is already within us, waiting to be expressed and emanated outward. This means that it is up to us to cultivate the love that is within and allow it to flow to our partners. If we feel we are not in love with our partner anymore, it means that when we focus on our partner we are not allowing the love from within us to flow. We have an association or belief about them that is inhibiting our own flow of love. Our true Self never stopped loving our partner, so when we don't feel love anymore it is only because we are not allowing our true Self to shine. This does not mean that every relationship should last forever. We can still love our partner and decide that it is time to move on from the relationship. In fact, it is to our advantage to continue loving the person because that is an indication we are aligned with our true Self. Paradoxically, the best thing we can do if we want to separate or divorce our partner is to love them first. If we are able to do this, it will be a clean separation (at least on our end) and we can move forward with our lives peacefully. If we separate with resentment or anger, we will carry these with us into the next phase of our lives.

Love in Education

This book is not about tackling the subject of our educational system. However, I would like to briefly comment on this topic because of its importance to the future of our world. Have you ever wondered why there is little or no place in our current educational system for a curriculum on love? Yes, love is difficult to define. Yes, there are many different views on this subject, depending on family, culture, etc. Yes, it may be challenging for us to agree on ways to present this material to students. Yet if we proclaim, as many of us do, that love is one of the most (if not the most) important aspects of our lives, why do we not create opportunities for our children to learn and discuss this important topic in a school setting? Years ago I worked for a start-up charter high school that offered weeklong enrichment classes. These were elective classes in addition to the primary curriculum that students could choose. I offered a class on the nature of love that many students chose because they were hungry for this type of learning. We had so many valuable discussions in that class, such as what it truly means to love another, the concept of "falling" in or out of love, the purpose of being in a relationship, etc. I believe our children are yearning for this type of learning, and finding a way to integrate it into formal education would help us shift the current paradigm.

Old Paradigm: If I just find the right person, then I will be complete and know how to love.

Enlightened Relationship: Love comes from within me, and I must cultivate it, nurture it, and allow it to be expressed in the world.

Chapter 3

The Enmeshment Virus
to
Self-Empowerment

While all relationships do not begin with a feeling that each person completes the other, as in the Jerry McGuire Syndrome, EVERY relationship (in which I am aware) has suffered to some degree from the Enmeshment Virus. In the old model we are taught, either implicitly or explicitly, that we are responsible for each other's feelings and that our partners are here to meet our needs. This starts at an early age when our parents or caregivers teach us that we need to behave in a certain way to please them or to prevent them from being angry, frustrated, etc. Please note that I am not condemning our parents for this conditioning. As a parent, I know firsthand how difficult it is not to do this to our children. I am guilty of conditioning my daughter in this way to an extent, although I am much more conscious of it now. Nevertheless, most of us are conditioned into this way of thinking and believe it to be a necessary aspect of relating to our partners.

We become enmeshed, or "entangled," with our partners by either believing they are responsible for our feelings or believing that we are responsible for theirs. Both ways present problems and we often move back and forth between the two. If we make our partners responsible for our feelings/experiences, we become disempowered. Now it is up to them to make us feel good, and if they don't do what we want, we will suffer. Any time we need our partners to be different in any way in order for us to feel better, the virus is active within us. It can be subtle and small or something seemingly significant. Many people will argue this point and say they are justified in feeling frustrated, angry, or sad because of the actions or inactions of their partner. This just further anchors the sense of disempowerment and powerlessness over our own emotional well-being. I am not suggesting that we "should not" feel badly in response to our partners, but just to recognize that when we do it is the Enmeshment Virus alive and well.

If we believe our partner's feelings are our responsibility, it will become our job to make them feel O.K. or to prevent them from getting upset. The tricky thing about this virus is that we are often not fully conscious of its presence. I never thought I would fall prey to it when I finally realized it was affecting me in a big way. My wife and I both do a lot of work from home. She, bless her heart, had a tendency to get very stressed while working (Universe, please note that I am using past tense!). Any number of things related to technology would set her off, such as the computer not working properly, the printer not functioning, not being able to figure out a particular piece of software, etc. This would (again Universe, pay attention; I am using the past tense) trigger me into stress or anger because unconsciously I thought it was my responsibility that she wasn't feeling well in that moment. I found myself often thinking about how to prevent my wife from getting upset. Rather than being inspired by love, I was being motivated by fear. This is living from the outside in rather than the inside out. In other words, it is worrying about what another will think first rather than listening to our own inner guidance.

We can, of course, influence the feelings of our partner. We can be inspired by love and do something that might help uplift them, such as completing a chore that is normally theirs, buying a small gift, writing a note of appreciation, taking them out, etc. But we don't do this because we believe we are responsible for their feelings; we do it because it is who we truly want to be in the relationship! We do it because it is an expression of our true Selves. This is love-inspired action. And of course, it is most effective when we can take this action without any expectations of a specific result. In a paradoxical way, our partner's reaction becomes "irrelevant" to our well-being. Maybe they will be uplifted, or maybe not. But we are doing it for the joy of expressing our love because this is who we want to be. This may sound like the strangest relationship advice you have ever heard, but never do anything FOR your partner ever again—do it because it is who you want to be.

Self-Empowerment

We are responsible for the way we experience the world. Period. This means that whatever we are thinking, feeling, or doing is up to us and we do not place the burden of responsibility on our partner. This is true self-empowerment. Notice I did not use the word "blame." Full acceptance of responsibility does not equal blame. We are responsible for our experience but we do not blame ourselves for reacting or feeling a certain way. This includes our thoughts and feelings about our partner. Regardless of what they do or don't do, we have the power to perceive them the way we choose. This can be difficult, of course, if we have developed a habit of reacting to them and seeing them as being responsible for how we are feeling. Nevertheless, if we react to our partner in frustration, anger, sadness, etc., it is our responsibility and we can begin to change this pattern one step at a time.

Our partner is responsible for their feelings and the way they experience the world as well. It is up to us to trust they are fully capable and have their own inner reSources to handle their emotional well-being. And this is true. They have their own true Self guiding them and loving them, and they can choose to align with it just as we can.

However, this is not a license to intentionally hurt the other or defend something we may have done. Sometimes after teaching this to couples they will use this principle against each other and in the middle of an argument exclaim, "I am not responsible for your feelings! Steve even said so!" The irony is that when we use the principle in this way, we actually do not believe it in that particular moment. There is often an underlying current of feeling responsible for the other and this is just a way of defending ourselves and preventing us from moving into deeper intimacy. Even though there is truth in the statement, it usually does not help in a discussion if we remind our partners that they are responsible for their own feelings. I have used this tactic in my own relationship on occasion, albeit more subtly, and it creates more distance than intimacy.

In fact, the only way to create true intimacy in a relationship is to take full self-responsibility and trust in our partner's ability to do the same. When we are able to achieve that state we can sit with our partner, even in their pain, and not take it on. Only then will we refrain from being reactive or defensive in our interactions. We can allow them to have their experience and feelings, whatever they may be, and maintain a deep connection with them.

If we are to use this principle in a healthy way, both partners will commit to self-responsibility. What would our relationships look like if we made this commitment? There would be complete ownership of our feelings, reactions, and experiences and therefore no need for blame. If we had a reaction to our partner's behavior, we would understand that the reaction is our own to resolve within ourselves. We may choose to discuss the matter, but both individuals would be self-empowered and all blame would dissolve into the ethers.

Old Paradigm: My partner is responsible for my needs and feelings (and vice versa).

Enlightened Relationship: I am fully responsible for my thoughts, feelings, and actions and I have the power to change them. I am Self-Empowered.

Chapter 4

Judgmentitis
to
Unconditional Love

When we judge or criticize our partner, whether verbally or just in our minds, we are infected with Judgmentitis, a.k.a. "Stink Eye," not to be confused with Pink Eye. This can be a judgment or criticism of any realm, such as our partner's physical appearance, parenting skills, ability to communicate, apparent emotional distance, neediness, work ethic, lack of helpfulness, and the list goes on. What qualifies the thought as a symptom of Judgmentitis is that we believe something *should not* be as it is, and we feel worse when we think it. If we think about an aspect of our partner that we don't like, or we think is not up to par, and it negatively impacts our own emotional state, we are engaging in Judgmentitis. The most important concept to understand about this is that these thoughts are toxic to us. They distance us from our own true Self and affect our well-being.

Let's say our emotional state of being is hovering around contentment and we think about our partner for whatever reason. Then we notice they have left their clothes on the floor. We think, "He is so messy." (Down the scale.) "Why does he always do this?" (Down the scale.) "I have asked him many times not to do that." (Down the scale.) "He must not care about me." (Down the scale.) We have just taken ourselves from contentment down to irritation or frustration, and if we continue on that train of thought, we may go all the way to anger. Our own thoughts have taken us away from love and joy, which is where we would prefer to be.

Emotional State of Being

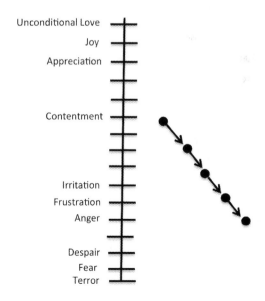

Unconditional Love
Joy
Appreciation

Contentment

Irritation
Frustration
Anger

Despair
Fear
Terror

But what if it's true? What if my partner really doesn't communicate effectively, or doesn't parent well, or doesn't help around the house? If the way we are thinking about our partner causes us to feel worse, then we are moving away from our true self--period. If we have developed a strong habit of judging our partners and find ourselves there often, we must find a way to change our perception if we want true fulfillment.

Our emotions are always the barometer for our alignment or misalignment to our true selves. I am not suggesting that we should be perfect and never judge or criticize, but just for us to understand that when we get stuck in it, we can use that feeling as guidance. Sometimes if we are feeling powerless we have to go through the feeling of blame in order to get to a higher state, but that is only a temporary "passing through." We can let ourselves move through that frequency and on to better feeling ones. Becoming skilled at the art of letting an emotion be, without feeding or resisting it, is extremely beneficial.

Many of us have been taught not to criticize our partner's character, but that it is appropriate and effective to notice and complain about their behavior. In other words, if we thought our partner was not helping out around the house enough we would not call them lazy, but we would complain they are not helping enough and tell them how we feel about it. On the surface this may seem like a good way of handling the situation. After all, don't we have to tell our partner how we feel about something so they know and can then make adjustments? Well, let's see what is happening at the metaphysical level.

The problem with this method is that very often when we complain about a behavior we are focusing energy toward something we do not prefer. We are actually energizing it and giving it more life by continuing to focus there. I learned a saying from an acupuncturist friend of mine that states, "Energy flows where attention goes." Therefore, if we continue to complain, whether to our friends or to our partner, we are inadvertently keeping the issue alive and well in our OWN experience. In addition, and this is extremely important to understand, when our emotional well-being is negatively impacted by noticing our partner's behavior, we are judging. Even if we try to separate their behavior from their character, we are still judging that something is wrong or inappropriate or shouldn't be so. We are still in the mindset that whatever they did should not have happened, and that is a judgment. In these moments, we are not loving our partners because we have moved away from the energy, or frequency of love. Therefore, to make a statement such as, "I still love you even though I am angry with you," does not compute—at least the way I am defining love. I am suggesting that love, in part, is a vibratory frequency that we are either resonating with or not in any given moment. We could say, "I am still committed to this relationship even though I feel angry at the moment," and that would be accurate. This concept applies to our children as well because we often tell them that we love them even though we are frustrated or angry with them. The truth is we are not in a state of love in those moments. Without even realizing it, we place all kinds of conditions on our love for our partners, our children, and ourselves through the virus of Judgmentitis.

In addition to being toxic to our own well-being, Judgmentitis serves another important function. When we judge another, it creates a wall or barrier that prevents us from being able to connect with them. If we judge, then we can easily keep our distance from the other and not have to risk intimacy. This often creates a fascinating feedback loop that keeps us stuck in place. Let us say that my desire is to feel close to my partner and have an intimate connection with them, yet I don't think they are trying hard enough to be available to me. So in my mind I begin to perceive them as not doing enough to connect with me. This might lead me to say things such as, "I want to connect with you, but you aren't being open enough," or "Why can't you just share your feelings with me?" With this mindset I am actually not allowing myself to connect with my partner. In my attempt to connect with them, I am actually blocking the very intimacy that I desire. It is important to understand that when making a request from my partner, I must be allowing/receiving the thing that I am requesting. Otherwise, I will not be available to receive it even if they are attempting to give it to me.

Unconditional Love

The online dictionary of Merriam Webster defines unconditional as "not limited in any way; complete and absolute." What does it mean to love unconditionally? It means that we allow our partners to be as they are without needing to change them, without **any** conditions. It means that when we put our attention on our partners, we feel love in our hearts; we vibrate in the frequency of love. We can see the divinity and perfection within them, regardless of outer appearances. In other words, we are at the upper end of the state of being when we think about them or see them. We may not always be able to do this, but it is what we are striving for. Why? Because we are made from the energy of unconditional love, so it is who we are at our core. When we love unconditionally we are expressing and allowing who we are at a fundamental level, which is why it feels so good. It is to our advantage to allow our partners the absolute freedom to be who they are. The opposite of unconditionally loving our partners is Judgmentitis, which is a form of resisting our true self. When we engage in Judgmentitis, we constrict ourselves and expend a great deal of energy.

Yes, it is a lofty goal to strive to love unconditionally, but that does not mean we should not hold it as our ideal. Most of us cannot stay in a constant state of unconditional love, but we can recognize when we are not there and then begin to consciously move back toward it. It is important to remember that the ego has many traps that attempt to move us toward fear rather than love. These ploys seem to become more and more subtle as we grow in our awareness. One of the more common traps is for the ego to ask questions such as, "What's in it for me? What am I going to get out of this?" Sometimes we may not be fully aware the ego is asking these questions, but they are often present, even if in the background of our consciousness. As soon as these questions are asked, we begin to inhibit our ability to love unconditionally. We must understand that loving unconditionally has nothing to do with what we are going to get from our partner. All concern about what we can get from them must be transcended. And the great paradox, of course, is that when we love unconditionally, without any thought of what are going to get, we open ourselves to receive the greatest of gifts. We unlock the door of our own heart to experience the glorious love of all creation.

Another common trap when we consider ourselves to be "spiritual" is to beat ourselves up when we do not love. "I have done so much personal work so I should be able to love unconditionally. What is wrong with me?" we may say to ourselves. Or we may pretend that we are loving when deep inside we are hurting or carrying resentment. It is important to be fully honest as to exactly how we are feeling. One of the quickest ways to begin to move toward loving our partners again is to have love and compassion for ourselves. We accept where we are in the moment, have compassion for ourselves, let go of resistant thoughts and begin to gently move toward loving our partners again. If we judge or criticize ourselves, we are by definition not in unconditional love. So very often the love must be turned toward ourselves first, which will free us to love our partners again.

See With the Eye of the Heart

There is an important clarification to the idea of allowing our partners to be themselves. It is not possible for us to allow our partners to be as they are if we keep focusing on aspects of them that we do not like. We cannot keep activating within us what we consider to be poor parenting skills, messiness, character flaws, etc., and still maintain a state of love. The paradox is to allow our partners to be as they are without dwelling on characteristics that we do not like. The way to achieve this is to see with the **eye of the heart**, which can penetrate the exterior shell and gaze directly into another's being. This eye is not fazed by any "character flaws" or "weaknesses" because it knows the unlimited potential that awaits actualization on the inside. It can see the beauty, the gifts, and the value inherent in the other, which may not even be visible to them. It's not that the eye of the heart is blind to "negative" traits, it just understands this is not who they truly are. In some ways, developing the eye of the heart is much like mastering a skill. There must first be a strong desire and intention to master it. Study, practice, and repetition are all necessary to strengthen this ability. And, of course, encountering many failures along the way will give valuable instruction where improvements can be made.

Practicing Forgiveness

One of the most important aspects of moving toward unconditional love is to fully repair after feelings have been hurt. Repairing in this way means that we are able to reconnect with our partner and feel a sense of love and appreciation for them again. It means that we can look into their eyes and feel intimately connected to them without any resistance. This requires the ability to truly forgive, which for many of us is the most challenging aspect of love. It seems so easy to hold on to resentment and anger, and so difficult to let go. Forgiveness is really an act of self-love because we are the ones letting go of the pain and returning to a state of love. I have found that the only way to move toward forgiveness is to care about myself so much that I am not willing to resent or hold on any longer. I get to a point where I cannot take what I am doing to myself any longer and have to find a way to let go.

There are many reasons we may choose not to forgive. One is the belief that by forgiving we are opening ourselves up to being hurt again. This is a very interesting protection mechanism, isn't it? We constrict ourselves and hold on to pain so that we won't get hurt. Fascinating! Another way we stay stuck is to not allow ourselves to feel anger. We stuff the anger down because it is too frightening for us. Once an emotion like anger has been born within us it is important to allow it to be. This doesn't mean we have to act it out and put the anger on someone else, but we must allow it within ourselves so that it can complete itself and flow out of us. This gives us the freedom to move toward love once again.

Another barrier to forgiveness is self-blame. This process is often unconscious but we blame ourselves or believe that somehow we deserved to be treated poorly. On the surface we may blame the other person but underneath we loath ourselves and hold on to that blame as a way to perpetuate the situation.

Death and Eternity as Allies to Love

What does death have to do with love? We can use the idea of death to love more fully. The main culprit that prevents us from loving without limits is fear. We are afraid of getting hurt or not being loved in return, and the list goes on. But when we embrace the inevitability of our own death, it can free us to love unconditionally. In this body and with this personality, we only have one life to live. What is there really to be afraid of then? Nothing! We are going to die anyway, so why not love with all of our heart in every moment? We can take advantage of the idea that our time in this body is limited, so we have nothing to lose.

Most of us really don't truly understand that we are going to die. Yes, of course, superficially we know that everyone dies and that we are going to die some day, but we really don't **know** it and love every day as if it was our last. One exercise I often give couples is to imagine that they knew that they were going to die in one year. I ask them to consider how they would live their life and what their relationship would be like with this knowledge. Most couples respond that they would love more, worry less, and have more fun in life. How would you live your life if this was your situation? Whether it is one year from now, two years, or thirty years, it is going to happen. We can use this knowledge in a positive way to live and love more fully.

Paradoxically, we can also use the idea that we are eternal beings to help us love unconditionally. The truth is that our spirit is eternal and will never die. In this sense, we are actually invincible. Nothing can "kill" our spirit or cause us to not exist, so there is nothing in which to fear. So why not love unconditionally? Again, we have nothing to lose but so much to gain.

Old Paradigm: Judging my partner's "faults" will get them to change. If I love unconditionally, I have to settle for things I don't like in the relationship.

Enlightened Relationship: Loving unconditionally creates the optimal environment for both of us to be our best selves.

Chapter 5

Mad Compromise Disease
to
We Can Both Have What
We Truly Want

In the old model of relating we operate from a very limited view of the world and ourselves. We often make the mistake of thinking that we must compromise our desires and ourselves in relationships. We have the mistaken notion that "compromising" is necessary in order to either demonstrate our love for our partner or to make the relationship function harmoniously. Mad Compromise Disease is probably the leading cause of resentment today. By compromise I am referring to when one person feels they have to give in or give up something and believes they will not be able to get what they desire. If we feel as though we are giving in, or doing something we really don't want to do, or not doing something we really wanted to do, all because it was what our partner wanted, we will become resentful. In addition, we will more than likely want our partner to be the one to compromise next time. And the disharmonious dance of quid pro quo begins.

This usually begins early on in the relationship and may be very subtle. When deciding on a restaurant, one partner agrees to the other's wishes but internally now feels slighted. When doing household chores, one partner believes they carry too much of the load but they continue to do it anyway. Or it may not be so subtle, such as when one partner takes an unfulfilling job because the other has fears about money. Whatever the reason, each time there is a compromise made we add a bit more resentment to the mix. The resentment, of course, is not just toward our partner but also toward us because of the lack of self-honor. It's as though we walk around wearing backpacks and for every compromise we add a rock of resentment to our own backpack. It gets heavier and heavier over time until we cannot carry it anymore.

Sometimes rather than being on the acquiescing side we will try to convince our partners to do something or agree to something that they do not want to do. We think that in order for our desire to be fulfilled they must do something even if they don't want to do it. Even if they agree unwillingly in the short term to do X, it will have unwanted repercussions for us. When we "force" the issue in this way it is usually not satisfying to us (even though we got our way), and we are actually decreasing the probability that our desire will be fulfilled in the future. Resentment will increase in them and they will likely dig in their heels even deeper next time, resisting even more.

When we are discussing matters with our partner and operating from this limited view, we often react emotionally out of fear that what we want will not be satisfied. We feel the need to defend or attack to try and get our way. Our ability to think clearly and creatively begins to decrease, and it becomes difficult to find a way for both parties to be satisfied.

We Can Both Have What We Truly Want

My desires are important. Your desires are important. We can both have what we want because the universe has the resources and ability to deliver to both of us what we truly desire. We do not need to compromise our desires or ourselves and neither does our partner. Think about what kind of relationship this would foster. We would know that each party was committed to the idea that both could get what they truly desired. There would be no reason to defend or attack because we know that in the end we both will be satisfied with the outcome. When discussing matters or trying to negotiate situations, we would be able to relax and stay at the upper end of the emotional scale. And when we are able to stay in a good feeling place, i.e. high vibration, we are able to think more creatively to solve the issues at hand. We have access to higher vibrational thoughts and we are allowing the universe to assist us. Sometimes the answers may not be immediately available, but that does not mean they won't come later. Even if it is not immediately clear how both desires can be fulfilled, never waiver from the knowledge that it will happen.

A key point to understand is that our desire may or may not come *through our partner*, especially initially. This is true even when it appears that my desire is directly related to my partner. We must give up the notion that we have to control how the Universe will lead us to our desire. At times it is helpful to go below the surface and identify the essence of the desire. What is it that I truly want? What is it that I want to experience? What is the feeling I will have when this desire comes to pass? Often when we go below the surface and look deeply at the desire there is a fundamental feeling we want to experience. Whatever the feeling, whether it is love, connection, joy, fulfillment, etc., we must give up the notion that it has to come exactly the way we think it should.

For example, let's say that I love to hike and I really want my partner to hike with me. My partner, however, hates hiking and resists my invitations. This could very easily become a point of contention if I continue to hold on to the idea that my partner "should" want to hike with me. If I recognize that what I really want is not just to hike but also to connect with my partner, I can find ways to do both. I can consult with my partner and brainstorm other ways we can connect that we both enjoy. And to satisfy my desire for hiking, I might find others to hike with who truly enjoy it.

The universe is so large, complex, and beautiful that we cannot even comprehend it fully. The Source that created this universe has infinite resources and wisdom. Do we really think that it cannot find a way to provide the two of us what we both desire? When we take a step back and look at the bigger picture, that faulty assumption is almost laughable. We can, along with the assistance of our Spirit, find a way that both of us can be satisfied with the outcome.

Old Paradigm: I must compromise myself in order to have a great relationship.

Enlightened Relationship: We can both have what we truly want.

Chapter 6

Disconnection Delusion
to
We Receive What We Give Out

Things just happen to me. Life is a matter of chance and luck. My state of being has no impact on my environment or my experience. I have no impact on how my partner treats me. These thoughts, beliefs, and attitudes are at the root of Disconnection Delusion. The delusion is that we are disconnected from others and the world around us.

From a global and environmental standpoint, Disconnection Delusion can be seen in the way we have sometimes treated Mother Earth. Not fully understanding our connection to the Earth and other living beings, we have done damage in many areas. In relationships, there is the delusion that our thoughts and feelings have no impact on our experience of others. On one side of the delusion we have the victim mentality. We believe we are the victims to the actions of others. Our partner treats us with disrespect or doesn't care about us, and we feel victimized. Complaining to friends and family members about our partner becomes a habit. We keep waiting for our partner to stop treating us so poorly, thinking that we are not connected or responsible in any way for what we are experiencing. We can become immersed in victim energy and feel isolated and alone.

On the other side of the delusion is the perpetrator mentality, where we feel it necessary to exert force or power over someone else. This is often our misguided attempt to repair our feeling of disconnection in some way. Very often we don't even realize we have become a perpetrator because our actions seem justified. I have caught myself on many occasions retaliating against my wife because in my mind "she started it." Therefore, I have the right to retaliate, don't I? So there I go, slipping right into a perpetrator role because I am feeling disconnected and disempowered. The truth is that the web of life connects her with me, just like all of us, so my actions toward her have a direct effect on me. In fact, what I do to her I am really doing to myself. What we do to anyone else we are doing to ourselves.

We Receive What We Give Out

As stated earlier, we are co-creating every experience we have with our partners. On an individual level, our beliefs, thoughts, and feelings become our experiences. This is how the universe operates and how we are designed. There is no exception to this metaphysical principle, including in our relationships. When loving thoughts are active within us, we transmit that to the universe and it comes back in our experiences. The more we focus on the best in our partners and keep those thoughts active, the more we will have experiences that demonstrate the best in them. The more we focus on negative aspects or faults in our partners, the more we will have experiences that match those thoughts. This is because *we receive what we give out.*

We are transmitting energy all of the time and communicating with our partners any time we think about them. Even if we don't use verbal communication, our partners are receiving the thought energy. This is not to say that they will act out every thought we have about them, but the more we think a certain way about them, the more likely we will experience them in that way. The universe operates in a very interesting dance of probabilities and possibilities. We do live in a realm of infinite possibilities, but as we think a certain way it guides the probability of our experiences. It is not until the moment of our experience that it becomes 100%. For example, if we are having judgmental and critical thoughts about our partner and we continue that line of thinking, we increase the probability that we will have an unwanted experience with them. This is because we are lowering our vibrational frequency as we think that way and we shift into a reality where those types of experiences reside.

Let us say that based on our current vibration we have a 50% chance of having an unwanted experience with our partner. Then we begin to focus on something we don't like about them and we think critical thoughts. As we continue to have these critical thoughts and feel worse, the probability of having the unwanted experience goes from 50% to 60% (these are arbitrary numbers). And if we continue even longer, the probability will rise higher - 70%, 80%, etc. Even if we try to fake it and pretend like we are feeling OK, we are still very likely to have an unwanted interaction with them. The energy we are in is negative and our partner is receiving it even if we don't say a word. We are transmitting these signals to them and increasing the chance that they will say or do something that "confirms" our critical thoughts.

Now let's say we look at the same situation all over again and our current vibration gives us a 50% chance of having an unwanted experience. This time we make a conscious choice to begin shifting our energy by focusing on characteristics we appreciate in our partner. So before interacting with them we begin to feel better and our train of thought about them has become more positive. The probability of having a positive experience begins to shift up from 50% to 60% to 70%, and if we keep activating those positive thoughts and feelings, the probability will continue to rise. It is important to emphasize that the thoughts of appreciation or compassion must be genuine for the probability to shift. Our emotions must be integrated with the thoughts of appreciation because that is the indication that our frequency is rising. Yes, I have now taken all the romance out of our interactions by breaking them down to probabilities and percentages!

Of course if we have deeply held limiting beliefs about our partner or our relationship, shifting in this way is not so easy to do. But all of life operates in this way because we are constantly transmitting thought energy to the universe and it responds accordingly. We could take any subject and begin thinking about it right now. The more we activate positive thoughts and feelings about that subject, the more probable we will have a positive experience regarding it. If we have a strong habit of thinking thoughts about that subject that do not feel good, we will have to work diligently to change the momentum because of the pattern we have developed. Remember, the universe gives us experiences that match the *essence* of our thoughts, which is why every thought does not enter our experience.

Years ago I began testing this idea out in my relationship, and the more I did, the more confirmation I received. Because this is so contrary to our current paradigm, which assumes that our beliefs, thoughts, and feelings have no direct impact on the external world, it is difficult to suddenly believe. It must be tested in the laboratory of your own relationship and life. So I encourage you to begin to be aware of the way you are thinking and feeling about your relationship and the types of experiences you are having. I am certain you will often find a correlation between the quality of your thoughts about your partner and the experiences you have with them.

When first attempting to implement the principle that *we receive what we give out* in a relationship, it can be easy to get discouraged. We can think that we have changed our own beliefs and vibration, and our partner may continue to engage in unwanted behavior and frustrate us. I have proclaimed to myself many times, "This law of attraction crap does not work! I have changed and she (my wife) is still doing the same old shit!" This is because I sometimes forget a very important paradox related to this principle. If we are trying to change, such as thinking more positively about our partner, in order to get them to change, it will not yield the results we are wanting. In fact, it will often backfire on us and cause more resistance and frustration. We must be shifting our vibration and cultivating loving thoughts because it feels good to us and because that is the kind of person we want to be. It cannot be an attempt to change them because we think they should be different in some way. If we are doing it in an attempt to change them it means we are not accepting the person as they are and, therefore, passing off a judgment. The Universe cannot be fooled because it knows our true vibration. It will sense the judgment (be it ever so slight) in our energy and give back to us what we are truly sending out.

Echo…Echo…Echo…

Have you ever yelled near a canyon or mountain range and heard the fascinating sound of your echo? The louder you yell, the more you hear the echo in return. The Universe has a very interesting echo effect that we can use as an opportunity to test ourselves. As mentioned above, sometimes we think we have transformed ourselves around a particular issue but the Universe will still send us the same type of experience. The key is to respond differently even when things look the same. If we react the same old way, in anger, frustration, discouragement, etc., then we really haven't changed and we will attract the same experiences. When we can respond differently, then we know we have truly changed and the Universe will respond in kind. If we can, it is best to say, 'Ah yes, this is just an echo from the past and an opportunity to respond the way I prefer.' Of course, the new response must include the way we are feeling and not just our outward behavior. Pretending to feel O.K. when we are really feeling discouraged does not work. Remember, the Universe is never fooled! It knows our vibration no matter how we look on the outside.

Where, Oh Where, Do They Come From? (Origin of Feces)

Okay, maybe it's a bit strong to call them feces, but why do we have all of these "crappy" limiting beliefs? When we are conceived, we begin to absorb the energy and belief systems of our parents. Initially, our mothers have the greatest impact because we are a part of the cells of her body, which are being informed by her energy field. Beginning at birth and throughout childhood, we are affected by the beliefs of our parents/primary caregivers. Because our psyche is more permeable when young, we take on many beliefs of those around us. This is all happening at the energetic level, whether we are conscious of it or not. We then begin to have experiences that reinforce these beliefs so that they become imprinted in our psyche. This is different than the commonly held notion that we create our beliefs based on our experiences. It is actually the reverse of that. The belief is already within us and we experience the world as a result of the belief. These experiences then serve as the reinforcement of the belief so that it becomes more "hard-wired" within us. Again, this is happening whether or not we are conscious of the belief or not. When we are young, we usually have no conscious understanding of our beliefs, but they are informing our lives nonetheless. Although I am using the word belief, it may be more accurate to say that it is a packet of energy stored in our personal mind.

This information is passed down, mostly unconsciously, from generation to generation. Our parents picked up many of their beliefs from their parents, who got them from their parents, and so on. There are often patterns in our ancestral consciousness that we have "inherited." Additional influences to these belief systems that are passed down include cultural beliefs, societal beliefs, and the mass consciousness of humanity. However, it is up to us to decide which beliefs serve us and which do not. We are not destined to continue repeating any pattern that we would like to transform.

It may be challenging to comprehend if you had a difficult childhood, but at the level of Spirit we knew this would happen. We chose our parents and the circumstances of our conception with full knowledge of the challenges we would face. We knew that if we tapped into our strength and courage, we could conquer these challenges and move from limitation to freedom.

That Annoying Mirror!

Shortly after our daughter was born, I began to experience what I considered to be criticism and a lack of support from my wife regarding my career efforts. For a while we were stuck in a pattern of conflict about this. After a great deal of self-reflection I realized that getting married and then having a child had activated many limiting beliefs within me. A limiting belief often becomes strongly active when we think about a desire that we really don't believe is possible for us to experience. It causes us to think about the lack of what we want rather than the presence of what we want.

Limiting beliefs are bundles of energy that act like bee hives. If the hive is stirred up, the bees get active and begin to swarm around the hive. The bees represent resistant thoughts that get active within our psyche. Even though I was unaware of it, I had many limiting beliefs associated with marriage and having a child. When I got married the hive was stirred up, and when our daughter was born it became a full-blown swarm. Some of these thoughts included fears of not being able to support my family, insecurity about my abilities, etc. As these thoughts became active within me, I began to transmit these signals to the Universe. Remember, we receive what we give out, so I began to receive from my wife exactly what I was thinking about; namely self-criticism, fears about money, and insecurity. I also began to perceive her as being critical and began expecting criticism from her, which further compounded the problem. I noticed that when I would begin worry about her criticism, I would inevitably experience that from her. Many times her words were not even critical, but I would still perceive and interpret them that way because I was looking through the lens of insecurity.

My wife and I agreed, albeit at unconscious levels, to participate in each other's reflections. Generally, couples spend so much time with each other that they inevitably become affected by the energy of their partner and "agree" to participate by being mirror reflections. Interestingly, many of my wife's limiting beliefs were activated when our daughter was born as well. Some of these included believing she had to bear the full burden of responsibility for the family, fears of running out of money, etc. Like many couples, our issues became a perfect match and we began attracting unwanted experiences from each other. When my self-doubt and limiting beliefs about earning money were active, her belief that she had to carry the burden and shoulder her fears alone would also be active. There was no amount of verbal communication that was going to resolve these matters. We tried every "communication tool" possible and we would still get stuck or become reactive. The only resolution was to understand that we had to transform our own consciousness and way of thinking by letting go of our own limiting beliefs. This would then change our vibration and the signals we were sending out. Once we changed our own state of being and the energy we were transmitting, we could then experience something different from each other.

My daughter was another excellent source of information and evidence that we are attracting our experiences. I came to realize that children are like vibrational (or mood) barometers. They tell you exactly where YOU are in terms of your emotional well-being. In a general sense I noticed that when I was in a good mood (higher vibration), my daughter would tend to be in a good mood, cooperate more easily, etc. And when I was in a bad mood she also tended to be in a bad mood and challenging to deal with. More specifically, when I was struggling with the fears of supporting my family she would do things such as cling to my leg when dropping her off at day care. This was often a frustrating experience because it would take me a long time to leave when I already believed I didn't have enough time. So there I was, struggling with the idea of supporting my daughter, and she decides to cling to my leg and prevent me from going to work. It was the perfect reflection of my internal experience! My daughter was just responding to my vibration and the thought signals I was sending out. When I was feeling confident and trusting in the Universe, she would rarely engage in behavior like that. Even if she did engage is such behavior I wouldn't experience it as a problem for me.

Survival of the Fittest

A limiting belief has one primary job—to survive by reinforcing itself. It will do everything in its power to ensure its survival and is relentless in its struggle. The way it does this is to project onto the world in various ways so that we have experiences to reinforce the belief. Beliefs often become multi-layered and stack upon each other to make them even more challenging to uproot. We often think we are just "observing" the world as it is, not realizing that we are creating it with our beliefs and thoughts.

For example, let us say I have an active limiting belief that I am unworthy of being loved, and I am not even conscious that I have this belief. Two things begin to happen. The first is that I am transmitting this signal to the Universe, and the second is that this belief becomes the filter through which I interpret experiences. If I am in already in a relationship, my partner will likely begin to unconsciously participate in reflecting this belief back to me. They may forget about our anniversary or begin to work more late hours because of job demands. I begin interpreting my partner's behavior as not caring. I notice they left dishes in the sink and believe they did it because they don't care about me. I notice they are spending more time at work and believe it is because they don't want to be with me. The more I interpret these events in this way the more likely I will continue to experience them in this manner, and thus the more these will occur. The signals I am sending out will get stronger and my partner will participate in this drama to a greater degree. Even if it started as my interpretation, rather than my partner actually not caring about me, eventually it can and often does lead to becoming a "truth." In other words, if I keep activating the limiting belief that I am unworthy of being loved, eventually my partner will stop caring about me, or have an affair, or any number of other possibilities that "prove" I am unworthy of love.

If I am single and have an active belief that I am unworthy of being loved, I will likely have other beliefs layered on top. For example, I might believe that it is extremely difficult to find a good person. I may come to believe the city I live in hardly has any single men/woman. I might find faults with every person I date and believe that no one is "good enough" for me. There are a multitude of thoughts and beliefs that can spring out from the primary belief of unworthiness, but all of them will keep leading me to experiences that reinforce that idea. The more we understand the structure of beliefs and how they shape our experiences the more we can transform them into those we prefer.

Which Tool Is Best?

There are many tools and techniques to explore and transform limiting beliefs. Whichever one sounds most appealing and we feel most attracted to is the one we should choose in that moment. The attraction is the indication that it is a vibrational match to us. This does not mean we always have to use the same tool. Tomorrow we may feel more aligned with a different modality because our vibration will be different. In fact, because we are changing all the time we will actually be a different person tomorrow. This concept is represented in Buddhist teachings by the analogy of using a raft to cross a river. Once one has safely reached the other side of the river with a particular raft, it is not advisable to try and carry the raft for the rest of the journey. It will very likely be heavy and cumbersome. If a river is encountered again, a new raft must be constructed with new materials. The new raft may contain similar material, but it depends on what is available at the new location. Likewise, it is not advisable to become attached to a particular method at the expense of our inner guidance and intuition. Just because a tool or technique has worked well in the past does not mean it will be the best choice right now. We must go within and make our decision based on what we feel in the present moment.

Shift into Neutral

One method to defuse the power of a limiting belief is the tool of neutrality. It is based on the premise that all circumstances and events are fundamentally neutral in and of themselves. There is nothing written in stone that says any event has to contain a certain meaning. We have the free will to choose what meaning we place upon it. As human beings we have been endowed with the ability to create the meaning in our own lives, and this is true for every experience we have. If we can see that all of our partner's actions or inactions are first neutral, we can then begin to place the meaning that we prefer on the situation. The meaning we give an event or circumstance determines the effect we will get out of it. This concept may be summarized in the following simple equations.

POSITIVE MEANING IN =
POSITIVE EFFECT OUT

Or

NEGATIVE MEANING IN =
NEGATIVE EFFECT OUT

If we are getting a negative effect from some situation, such as an uncomfortable emotional reaction, it means that we injected a negative meaning into it. We can then self examine to discover exactly how we were defining that situation, and from that determine what we would prefer to experience. This kind of "negative" experience can be incredibly valuable because it helps us clarify what we truly desire for our lives.

"Core" Beliefs

Despite how relentless a limiting belief may be, please remember that it is not our Core belief. At our core, we know that we are unlimited beings with infinite potential. We know that we are lovable and capable of unconditionally loving another. We know that we are worthy of love and worthy of experiencing a truly remarkable relationship. These are Core beliefs because they express who we truly are. Remember, we have two selves, our true Self and the personal self. Our personal self will often cling to limiting beliefs because it perceives these are less painful than the alternative. This may not be true, of course, but the perception that holding on to the limiting belief will be less painful keeps it in place.

Ultimately, our limiting beliefs will be transcended and we will realize who we are. Even if we don't transcend them all in this life, we will make the realization when we transition to the spirit world in our death. The hero, and we are all heroes, always prevails no matter how many obstacles and challenges are faced. We will eventually realize our greatness. But why wait until death? Why not realize and live the truth of who we are in this life?

We are a vibrational match to everything we experience from our partners. We are resonating at a particular frequency that attracts or creates a certain experience from them. I cannot emphasize this point enough. We can't experience something if we are not resonating at the same frequency. When we are resonating at the frequency of love then we can experience love from our partner. If both partners understood this concept and did their best to apply it, their relationship would truly be remarkable. They would place a priority on the way they were thinking and feeling in order to send and receive the most positive energy possible. If they did experience something unwanted from their partner, they would know that it was just a reflection of their own beliefs and thoughts. They would see the experience with their partner as just an indication of their own vibration. They could then begin redirect their focus in a way that helped them feel better and shift their vibration, which would in turn result in more positive experiences with their partner. They would know that to get stuck in blame, either toward themselves or their partner only elicits more of the same experiences.

Old Paradigm: My thoughts and feelings have no impact on what I experience from my partner and the world around me.

Enlightened Relationship: My beliefs, thoughts, and feelings are transmitted to the Universe and reflected back to me through my partner.

Chapter 7

Purpose Deficiency Disorder
to
Joyful Co-Creation

We have all heard of the infamous ADD, but do you know about PDD? Many of us enter relationships without considering the real purpose of being in a relationship. We may be following societal norms without giving thought to the true function of a relationship. Or we may have given it some thought and started with direction and purpose in our relationship, but it was lost over time. Both of these are characteristics of Purpose Deficiency Disorder (PDD). When we lose sight of our purpose or if we never had one to begin with, it is easy to become distracted or get lost at sea. Without purpose, we don't see a bigger picture and minor situations can easily become major problems.

One of the major symptoms of PDD today is that the grass always seems greener on the other side. Rather than making the effort to appreciate what we do have or to change our current relationship, we begin to look elsewhere for fulfillment. Without a true sense of purpose, we think that being with someone else will be better because our current problems will not exist. And the grass usually looks so green over there, doesn't it? It's new and exciting and surely they will listen to me, unlike my current partner. Surely they won't be so messy, won't work such long hours, won't criticize me, and surely they will give me what I need. So we begin to check out and not do our best in the current relationship, sometimes leading to secret affairs. As I mentioned before, I am not suggesting that every relationship should last forever, but it is to our advantage to do our best in the current situation.

We will only feel fulfilled if we are doing our best and making the most out our current situation. In fact, the quickest way out of something unwanted is to feel as good as possible while still in it. The universe is responding to our vibration, and our emotions indicate how aligned we are in any given moment. The more aligned we are the more likely the Universe will show us a clear path. This doesn't mean that we keep focusing on negative aspects of the current situation. It means that we find a way to focus on our current situation that feels self-empowering. If we decide to pursue that other green grass covertly and without integrity, it will be difficult to feel good. Why not just tell our partners the truth? If we decide at some point that we want to leave the relationship, then we communicate it to our current partner. If we want to go outside our current relationship for sex or anything else, we discuss it with our partner first. This would be operating with courage and in complete integrity. There are way too many of us who stay in relationships because of the children, finances, or any other justification, and end up secretly straying because we are afraid to tell our partners the truth.

Joyful Co-Creation

What is the purpose of being in a relationship? Very often, we haven't even considered this question or have forgotten the reasons we entered the relationship. It is extremely beneficial to answer this question along with our partners, regardless of how long we have been together. Whether we have been together for many years or the relationship is brand new, it is valuable to take the time to consider this question for ourselves and then share with each other. For any pursuit in life, it is critical to discover and clarify the reason we are engaged in it.

One of the most exciting reasons to be in a relationship is to joyfully co-create together. Having this intention with our partners will serve us in many ways. How much fun can we have as we joyfully co-create our lives? What do we want our family life to look like? Our sex life? Our home? Let's co-create our next vacation together. What other experiences do we want to have together? It can be quite liberating to think of our relationship in these terms. Partners can work together in a co-creative process to have the life experiences they desire, supporting and inspiring the best in each other.

As individuals, we are here to create, pursue our passions, and express our gifts in the world. Therefore, at some level, the relationship must be a vehicle to support the expression and fulfillment of these individual desires as well as provide an opportunity for the couple to joyfully co-create together. This is important no matter what the individual desires may be. Whether the desire is to be a stay at home parent, to create a thriving business, to be an artist, to be a volunteer at school, etc., the relationship fosters the best in the individual. In any endeavor there are countless ways to be creative and use our gifts, and we will be better able to do that if the relationship supports it.

In the ideal situation, there is a harmonious balance of these individual pursuits and the shared goals of the couple. When the couple is working together on their shared goals they will be more powerful and successful. The energy of two moving in the same direction is much stronger than splitting the energy and going in different, and sometimes even competing directions. Because our desires change over time, it is important to clarify and address them on a continual basis with our partners.

The Sacred Journey

You and your partner have chosen to share a voyage together in this life. Think about the magnitude and importance of this statement. Out of all the people in the world, which is now over 7 billion, you chose each other with which to co-create. It doesn't matter how long you have been together or whether the relationship has presented challenges or not (and they all do), you have shared a portion of your lives together. That *is sacred*. You have given each other the opportunity to discover and become more of your true Selves. What an incredible gift you have given each other! Even if you decide to leave this relationship, you have still shared your journey together, and it is important not to negate its value and importance. Regardless of what has happened, you can use the experience as a valuable springboard to propel you toward the next leg of your journey. Finding positive meaning and the gifts from the relationship will help clear the way for your future, whether that includes being with your partner or not.

Old Paradigm: It is not important to understand purpose in a relationship.

Enlightened Relationship: Clarifying purpose and intention builds a solid foundation for the relationship to thrive.

Chapter 8

Embracing the New Frontier

We are living in exciting times! It has been suggested that the year 2012 marked a tipping point for humanity, wherein the collective consciousness of mankind is now more positive than negative. In addition, the creative energy of our world is flowing faster and at a higher frequency. Systems that do not have a positive orientation, meaning that they foster segregation, disharmony, separateness, dis-ease, etc., are now more likely to dissolve. New paradigms that are built on the foundation of love, oneness, and harmony will replace the old systems. In addition to economic, political, educational, agricultural, and health systems, our model of relationship is another such system that needs replacing, and it is up to us to lead the charge. If we continue to follow the wisdom and love of our true Selves, we will move in the right direction.

The truth is that we not only come from the same nonphysical energy, but we are all a part of one being—creation itself. We are all just different cells in the body of creation, carrying out different functions and possessing unique gifts. Each of us is an essential component of the whole. From this perspective our partner is just another aspect of us, playing a vital role in the game of Life. Desiring the best for them is the equivalent of desiring the best for us, because we are all a part of the same being. Can you feel the truth in this statement? Does your soul resonate when you think about this idea? Even as I write this, I can hardly contain the ecstasy I feel because I know it to be true for me.

Do you see the best in your partner? Do you believe in them? Do you see the divinity within them? Do you trust that they have all the resources of their higher Self within them? Do you see them with the *eye of the heart*? If you answered no to any of those questions, what are you waiting for? Your partner can only show you what you are willing to see. You must be willing to see all of these attributes in them or they will never be visible to you. This is the moment to begin, right now, and this moment is where all of your power exits. You can begin to create an Enlightened Relationship together and live your potential as individuals and as couples, fulfilling your personal dreams and co-creating glorious lives together. I for one will do my absolute best to live and teach these principles every day. Will you joy-n-me?